Pope John

D0115278

REV. JUDE WINKLER, OFM Conv.

Imprimi Potest: Michael Kolodziej, OFM Conv., Minister Provincial of St. Anthony of Padua Province (USA)
Nihil Obstat: Rev. James M. Cafone, M.A., S.T.D., Censor Librorum
Imprimatur: ✠ **Most Rev. John J. Myers, J.C.D., D.D.**, Archbishop of Newark

The Nihil Obstat and Imprimatur are official declarations that a book or pamphlet is free of doctrinal or moral error. No implication is contained therein that those who have granted the Nihil Obstat and Imprimatur agree with the contents, opinions or statements expressed.

© 2005 by CATHOLIC BOOK PUBLISHING CORP., Totowa, N.J.
Printed in Hong Kong   ISBN 978-0-89942-538-2

2

The Birth of Karol Wojtyla

POPE John Paul II was born in a small town near Krakow, Poland, on May 18, 1920. He was the second son of Emilia and Karol, an officer in the Polish army. The baby was baptized a little over a month later on June 20 and given the name Karol (which, in English, would probably be translated Carl or Charles).

There was a certain amount of sadness in his early life. His mother died when he was only eight years old, and his older brother Edmond died when he was twelve. Young Karol, though, was supported by a loving father. His father's wonderful example of faith also taught him to rely upon God. Young Karol remembered waking up from sleep and looking over and seeing his father on his knees in prayer.

In these early years he also developed a strong devotion to our heavenly Mother. Like most Catholics in Poland, he made a pilgrimage to the shrine of the Black Madonna. He was fifteen when he was admitted to the Society of Mary.

Young Karol also began to show what later became a life-long interest in theater. It was during high school that he acted in his first play. He himself would later write a number of plays.

The Nazi Invasion of Poland

KAROL began his university studies in Krakow when he was eighteen years old. He studied philosophy and literature.

These studies came to a sudden end when the Nazis invaded Poland on September 1, 1939. They almost immediately closed down the university, sending most of its professors to prison.

The Nazi occupation was very, very cruel. Many people were arrested simply because they were either educated or leaders in society. Most of them were never seen again.

Karol had to find a job so that he would not be arrested and sent away to do slave labor. He found a job in a quarry where he and others had to work very hard. After a while, he was transferred to work at a chemical plant.

Still, while doing this difficult work, Karol continued his studies by reading books on his own. He often recalled how his co-workers would let him read even while he was on the job. He also joined a theater group that performed plays in people's private apartments. This was dangerous, for if the Nazis had ever found out about what he was doing, they would probably have arrested him.

6

Karol's Spiritual Growth

EARLY in 1941, Karol's father died. He was now on his own during this horrible time.

The difficulties of this period did not shake Karol's faith. On the contrary, something very special was happening in his heart.

One great influence in his spiritual growth was a tailor named Jan Tyranowski. He was a layman who had read and studied the writings of the Carmelite Saints Teresa of Avila and John of the Cross. Karol was deeply moved by their teachings. From that time on, he wore a scapular (a devotion taught by the Carmelites).

More and more, he felt a call to the priesthood. The problem was that the Nazis had closed down the seminary. He spoke to various priests, then to the Archbishop and, finally, he began his studies on his own. Though working full time, he would read before and after work and sometimes when he could take a break during his workday.

Early in 1944, Karol was hit by a car while he was trying to save another person's life. He was in the hospital for two weeks.

Later that year, the seminary in Krakow reopened, and he was able to begin studying full time.

From Young Priest to Bishop

ON November 1, 1946, Karol Wojtyla was ordained a priest. Only two weeks later, his Archbishop sent him to Rome to continue his studies at a university called the Angelicum. He earned his doctorate degree there in June 1948.

He returned to Poland where he became an assistant pastor. While working in various parishes, he also continued his studies, earning another doctorate.

In 1953, he began to teach in the Catholic University found in Krakow. Later, when the Communists closed the university, he taught at the seminary and at the Catholic University in Lublin (another Polish city).

He also was a chaplain for university students and health-care workers. He showed his concern for their spiritual needs by the things he wrote about during this period. One of those writings, *Love and Responsibility*, spoke of how a man and a woman should express their love for each other in marriage.

Father Wojtyla became an auxiliary Bishop in Krakow in 1958. These were not easy years for priests and Bishops in Poland, for the Communists made practicing religion as difficult as possible.

The Bishop Becomes a Cardinal

BISHOP Wojtyla soon proved himself to be very talented at defending the needs of the Church in a way that did not enrage the Communists. He also served people in a most caring manner.

This is why he was placed in charge of the Archdiocese of Krakow in 1962 when its Archbishop died. Although temporary, the appointment became permanent when he was named as the new Archbishop of Krakow in 1965.

As Bishop, he attended the Second Vatican Council, which ran from 1962 to 1965. With his great learning and wisdom quickly recognized, he was asked to work on a number of documents, including one on the Church in the modern world.

Pope Paul VI acknowledged his talent and his contributions at the Council by naming him a Cardinal in 1967. Cardinals, advisors to the Holy Father, choose the next Pope when one dies.

As a Cardinal, he was responsible not only for his own archdiocese but also for Catholics throughout the world. He traveled to different continents to attend meetings, give speeches, explain to outsiders the difficulties of the Church in Communist lands, and to learn from the countries that he was visiting.

Pope John Paul II

IN August of 1978, Pope Paul VI died. Cardinal Wojtyla traveled to Rome, along with Cardinals from all over the world. Cardinal Luciani was elected Pope, and he took the name Pope John Paul I (after the names of the two previous Popes: John XXIII and Paul VI). Pope John Paul I, however, died after only 33 days, and the Cardinals gathered together again to elect a new Pope.

On October 14, the Cardinals prayed for guidance from the Holy Spirit, and two days later, they elected Cardinal Karol Wojtyla as the 264th Pope of the Roman Catholic Church. He took the name "Pope John Paul II" in honor of the Pope who had served before him.

Every Pope for the past 400 years had been Italian. When John Paul II came to the window of St. Peter's Basilica to speak to the crowd below in St. Peter's Square, he announced that he had come from a distance. He asked the people there to help him with his Italian if he made any mistakes.

On October 22, Pope John Paul II received his pallium, a type of stole worn by shepherds. Like St. Peter who was asked to care for the sheep in the Gospel of John, so Pope John Paul II was becoming the chief shepherd of the Church.

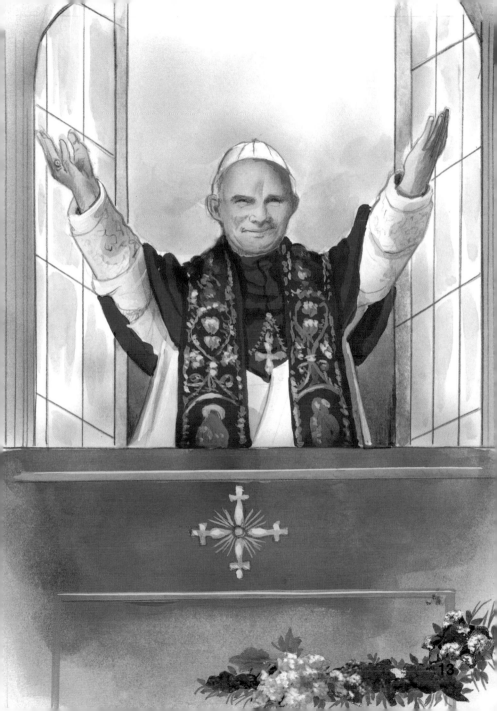

The Writings of Pope John Paul II

BEFORE he was elected Pope, John Paul had written many poems, plays, and books. From the very beginning of his papacy, Pope John Paul II used his talent as a writer to produce a series of documents to teach the faithful about our religion.

Pope John Paul II wrote about Jesus the Redeemer, God the Father, and God the Holy Spirit. He wrote about the Blessed Virgin Mary for whom he had a great devotion. He wrote about the Sacraments of the Eucharist and Reconciliation. He also wrote many letters to promote the value of the truth and to foster respect for life.

During his papacy, Pope John Paul II also oversaw the publication of two very important books that help guide the Church. The first is called the *Code of Canon Law,* a collection of all of the laws of the Church. Over time some of these laws had become confusing or were outdated. Thus, the Pope called for a new collection to guide the Church.

The other is called the *Catechism of the Catholic Church.* This is a collection of all the things we believe about our Faith regarding God, the Church, the Sacraments, the Angels and Saints, heaven, hell, and purgatory, and many other things.

The World Traveler

POPE John Paul II wanted to meet people to teach them about the Faith and to learn from them about their needs.

The Pope is the Bishop of Rome. Almost immediately after becoming Pope, he began to visit the parishes of his diocese. He met with many of the organizations in the parish, celebrated Mass with as many people as possible, and offered everyone greetings and teachings.

Pope John Paul II also traveled to his larger flock, making over 100 trips to foreign lands. Some of his visits were great celebrations of joy, especially when he traveled to his homeland of Poland.

Other trips were a bit more difficult. He traveled to countries still ruled by the Communists, such as Cuba. He also visited some countries that are mostly Orthodox Christian, such as Romania and the Ukraine. In the past, Catholics and Orthodox did not always get along, but he worked to make peace with the leaders of the Orthodox Churches. He also visited countries where the number of Catholics is very small.

On all his visits the people rejoiced, listened to what the Pope said, and went home with new insights into their Faith.

The End of Communism

WHEREVER the Pope went, he defended the dignity of each human being. People listened to his words, and they began to ask themselves whether their societies respected that dignity.

In Communist countries, the people realized that there was something very wrong with the way they were being governed.

Shortly after the Holy Father visited Poland as Pope for the first time, a movement arose to fight for the rights of every citizen. It was called Solidarity. It began as a labor union, an organization that defended the rights of workers, but it quickly took on greater responsibilities.

The fight for freedom was not always easy. For a while, the army took over Poland to keep the Communists in power. But, by 1989, the people's desire for freedom had become more and more powerful. In that year, country after country threw off the Communist yoke and became free.

A great sign of this peaceful revolution was the Berlin Wall tumbling down. The wall had been built by the Communists to keep people from escaping to freedom. Now people could travel where they wanted, practice their religion freely, and say what they wanted without being arrested.

The Pope Almost Dies

POPE John Paul II paid a great price for his courage and honesty. On May 13, 1981, an assassin named Ali Agca shot the Holy Father.

To this day, it is not clear who was behind this assassination attempt. Some people believed that it was the Communists who were trying to stop the Pope from giving hope to people.

The Holy Father was seriously wounded and almost died. He credits his survival to the intercession of Our Lady of Fatima, for he was shot on her feast day.

Many years later, the Holy Father revealed that certain world events had been foretold. The Blessed Virgin Mary had appeared to three young children in Fatima, Portugal, in 1917. She had revealed to them three secrets. The first two involved the rise of Communism and the death and destruction caused by the two World Wars.

The third secret was a prediction of the attempt to kill the Pope. The children saw a Bishop dressed in white and covered in red blood.

When the Holy Father recovered, he forgave the man who had tried to kill him.

21

Devotion to the Blessed Virgin Mary

THE Holy Father expressed his devotion to the Blessed Virgin Mary in many ways.

From his youth, he had visited many shrines dedicated to Mary. He would pray there for our Lady's love and protection. He continued this practice during his papacy, visiting almost every important Marian shrine throughout the world.

He also wrote an encyclical about the Blessed Virgin and her place in the life of the Church. Many of his other writings also include sections that speak about the importance of Mary in the history of salvation and in each of our own prayer lives.

In 2002, he proposed five new Mysteries for the Rosary: the Luminous Mysteries.

For many centuries there had been only fifteen Mysteries. While often considered a devotional prayer to Mary, the Rosary actually shows how Mary points to her Son, Jesus, for He is to be the Center of our lives and our love. The five new Mysteries that recall Jesus' public ministry emphasize this aspect of the Rosary even more. They are the Baptism of Jesus, the Wedding Feast of Cana, the Proclamation of the Kingdom, the Transfiguration, and the Eucharist.

Saints and Blesseds

THE Holy Father taught that all people are called to holiness. One way he did this was by beatifying and canonizing more people than all the other Popes combined between 1594 and 1978.

Beatification is the step before someone is declared to be a Saint. The Church investigates all of the teachings of the person being considered, making sure that all of them are faithful to the Church's teachings. In addition, the Church examines the person's reputation and requires that two miracles be performed through the person's intercession.

Through canonization the Church officially declares a person to be a Saint. There must be one more miracle after beatification for this to occur.

St. Maximilian Kolbe, one of the Pope's first canonizations, died giving his life for another prisoner in a Nazi prison camp during World War II.

The Pope also canonized Padre Pio, a Capuchin Franciscan friar who had borne the wounds of Jesus on his hands, feet, and sides for fifty years.

He also beatified Mother Teresa of Calcutta, who cared for the poor and dying in India for many years.

25

Holy Years

A NOTHER way that the Holy Father taught about holiness was to declare Holy Years to celebrate Christ as our Redeemer, the birth of the Blessed Virgin Mary, and the Jubilee Year of 2000.

The Holy Year tradition dates back to the Old Testament. Every seventh year, the Jewish people celebrated a sabbatical year when they would forgive debts and not plant crops. Then, every fifty years, they celebrated a Jubilee Year in which they would forgive more debts, return land to its original owners, and free their slaves.

In the modern era, there is a Holy Year celebrated every twenty-five years, during which pilgrims come from all over the world to pray in Rome. Once in a while, the Holy Father also calls a special Holy Year.

The first Holy Year that Pope John Paul II called was in 1983 to celebrate the 1950th anniversary of Jesus' death and Resurrection.

The second Holy Year, in 1988, celebrated the 2,000th anniversary of the birth of the Blessed Virgin Mary.

The third Holy Year, in 2000, marked the beginning of the new millennium.

World Youth Day

FROM the day that Pope John Paul II was ordained a priest, he always had a special ministry to young people.

This is why the Holy Father began a new tradition: World Youth Day. Young people from all over the world would come to spend a few days of prayer and teaching with the Holy Father.

The enthusiasm of the young people who attended was remarkable. They often had to sleep in tents in the middle of fields. They did not have the best food to eat. It was often rainy or hot. Yet, they spent day and night praying and singing and sharing stories of the Faith.

There also was joy on the Holy Father's face when he participated in these events. Even when he was tired or ill, he would light up with a grin every time that he met young people.

One time he came together with a group of young people who were hockey players. He took his crozier (the staff he carries) and held it like a hockey stick.

Whenever he spoke to young people, he reminded them of their duty to live the Gospel and to reject the false values of today's world.

Ecumenism

POPE John Paul II also reached beyond the confines of the Church to our brothers and sisters who believe in Christ and to those who believe in God but not in Christ.

He reached out to the Jewish people in a special way, having known many Jewish people while he was growing up in Poland. During the war, he helped save some Jewish people from the Nazis.

When he was a Bishop, he visited the chief rabbi in Krakow and visited the synagogue there.

Then, as Pope, he reached out to the Jews in many ways. He visited their synagogue in Rome. He commemorated the sufferings of the Jewish people during World War II by visiting the death camps in Germany and Poland and the memorial in Israel for those who died during World War II.

Pope John Paul II also met with leaders of the Anglican Church, the Lutheran Church, and many other Christian communities.

Several times during his papacy, the Holy Father also invited leaders of the world's religions to Assisi, Italy, to pray for peace. Assisi is the birth place of St. Francis of Assisi who is a symbol of the quest for peace and understanding among peoples.

The Pope's Illnesses

ONE of John Paul's most important teachings was that of the sanctity of life from the moment of its conception until one's natural death.

He also gave great witness to this teaching in his own life. Many times he was ill or injured, and yet he bore these difficulties with great dignity, offering up his sufferings for the Church.

Even in his old age, when he was very limited by illness, he still served the Church with great courage. He gave an example to the world of the dignity of those who are weak and broken.

Pope John Paul II went home to our Lord on April 2, 2005.